COCKTAILS

MORE THAN 80 SPARKLING IDEAS

COCKTAILS

MORE THAN 80 SPARKLING IDEAS

MURDOCH BOOKS

contents

ready, set, shake! Life isn't always a smooth ride, but luckily there's a chill-out lounge called the cocktail bar. To step into the sleek, sexy world of cocktails is to enter a zone of ageless glamour, where the

mind unfrazzles, tensions unravel and the senses soak up a multitude of sins. Slip on some sultry music, slide into something slinky and ponder again that eternal question: shaken or stirred?

notes for the lounge lizard

Cocktails are synonymous with glamourpusses, urban sophisticates and the cosmopolitan set, and with every single sip we cannot help but luxuriate in these glittering associations. From their rustic beginnings masking fiery bootleg liquor, cocktails are now on the cusp of a golden age, with spirit producers infusing classic spirits such as gin, vodka and tequila with exciting new flavours, promising infinite possibilities for those seeking the latest cocktail sensations.

There's no special mystique involved in cocktail making. It is an easy art to master and with a little dedicated practice you'll be serving drinks with flair and panache. All you need are a few simple implements, some basic ingredients, a steady hand, a highly developed sense of fun and a rampant imagination.

There's a cocktail in this book to suit any mood or occasion, from the snootiest soirée to splashing poolside frolics, smashing parties and after-dinner meltdowns. We'll even show you how to infuse spirits and whip up fruit purées for special 'signature' cocktails.

Before starting, a few quick words. Our recipes use a 20 ml (4 teaspoon) tablespoon, so if yours is a 15 ml (3 teaspoon) tablespoon, add an extra teaspoon per tablespoon. Recipes make one cocktail unless stated otherwise, using fresh, ripe fruit and fresh fruit juices unless otherwise specified. Finally, remember that although they may taste innocent, cocktails are highly intoxicating. So if you're hosting a cocktail party, offer plenty of food and non-alcoholic refreshments so your guests will remember what a fabulous time they had!

the bar essentials

You don't need truckloads of fancy implements to create a classy cocktail, and most of them you'll find lurking somewhere in your kitchen.

One implement you'll definitely need to buy if you don't already have one is a cocktail shaker, available in two basic types. A standard shaker usually has three stainless steel pieces: a canister that holds the ice, a lid with an inbuilt strainer that seals tightly over the top, and a twist-off cap. The Boston shaker often has a mixing glass as its base, snugly overlapped by a stainless steel top. It doesn't have an inbuilt strainer, so you'll need a separate strainer to filter the drink during pouring. The most widely used is a hawthorn strainer, which has a distinctive circular head with a spring coil that fits sweetly around the metal half of a Boston shaker.

The other major implement most budding cocktail stars will need is an **electric blender**. If you're a total fanatic, invest in a heavy-duty model with a powerful motor and sturdy blades that can cope with whole ice cubes (check the manufacturer's instructions). If your blender is a little lightweight, you'll need to crush the ice cubes before putting them in the blender. To help your blades last longer, add the liquid ingredients to the blender first, then the ice.

Next, find yourself a large **jug** or pitcher with a pouring spout to use as a mixing glass; this is especially useful for making multiple quantities of mixed drinks. You'll also need **measuring spoons** and a **jigger** for measuring alcohol. Jiggers usually have double-sided cups, one holding 15 or 30 ml (½ or 1 oz), the other holding 45 or 60 ml (1½ or 2 oz).

A long-handled bar spoon (preferably stainless steel) is used for stirring cocktails and 'floating' ingredients in layered drinks. It can also be used for 'muddling' fruit and herbs, or you could buy a special muddler, which is essentially a wooden pestle, from specialist kitchen stores.

Ice, ice and more ice is essential to a cool cocktail, so you'll need plenty of ice-cube trays, an ice bucket for storing ice cubes, and a pair of tongs or an ice scoop for dispensing ice — never use your hands!

Other bits and bobs include a citrus squeezer, chopping board, sharp fruit knife, sharp vegetable peeler and zester. For those finishing touches, stock up on plain and coloured toothpicks, pretty cocktail umbrellas, swizzle sticks and straws of all description.

glass class

Purists will insist on using the right glass for every drink. Short mixed drinks 'on the rocks' are served in an old-fashioned glass or tumbler; long mixed drinks are shaken, stirred or built in a highball glass or in a slightly deeper Collins glass. Cocktails without ice are poured into stemmed glasses to keep hot hands away from the drink. 'Short' drinks such as martinis are served in a triangular cocktail or martini glass. Champagne cocktails and some wine cocktails use a champagne flute, while cocktails containing egg yolks are usually dished out in goblets. Mixed or blended drinks are often served in a tulip-shaped glass. Other glasses include shot glasses, brandy balloons (enormous bowled glasses for swirling, sniffing and swilling fine brandies) and the sour glass, which resembles a champagne flute but has a shorter stem.

tricks of the trade

Here's a **really cool tip** for making a really cool cocktail: have everything **blisteringly cold**. Chill all your ingredients before using, and chill the glasses too, or leave a scoop of ice in them while preparing your drinks. Always use **fresh ice** for each drink, and the best ingredients you can source. Have all ingredients **ready to go** before you start mixing, shaking, stirring or building your drinks, and **don't overfill** shakers or mixers. To avoid spillage, never fill a glass to the brim, and remember to leave room for the **garnish**. When serving a cocktail, present the glass by its base or stem so you don't put hot, sticky handprints all over it. Finally, make each drink to order, as cocktails lose their 'verve' over time. On the following pages are some techniques you'll find handy.

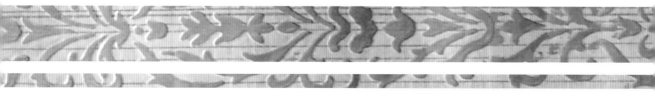

Crushing ice Firmly wrap some ice cubes in a dry, clean tea towel and gently clobber them with a mallet or whack them against a solid bench. Bash up a big batch and stash it in the freezer.

Blending Purée the cocktail ingredients in a blender to a smooth, drinkable consistency, but don't overblend or you'll have a weak, watery concoction. Unless you have a heavy-duty blender, use crushed ice rather than ice cubes in your blender.

Shaking Half-fill the cocktail shaker with crushed ice, add the other ingredients and vertically shake the canister vigorously until the shaker is frosty outside (10 seconds should do, but if your cocktail is very creamy or syrupy you might need to double the time). Strain into a chilled glass. Carbonated drinks should never be shaken or they'll lose their fizz.

Stirring For sparkling clean looks, certain cocktails are stirred in a mixing glass or jug with a handful of ice cubes. This chills the alcohol quickly, without diluting it. The cocktail is then strained into a glass.

Floating Gently pour the liqueur or spirit into the glass over the back of a spoon. Add the ingredients in the order specified in the recipe and do not mix — the idea is to create a layered effect.

Muddling Grind, crush or mash fresh fruit or herbs with sugar (usually in a cocktail shaker) using a muddler or bar spoon to release all the flavours.

Adding egg white Slide an egg white into a small glass receptacle and use a sharp knife to 'cut' or slice away a portion of egg white to slip into your drink.

Snazzy ice cubes Freeze fruit juice in an ice-cube tray, perhaps with some mint leaves or diced fruit.

some classic twists

Many recipes in this book will mention any garnish traditionally used to grace a particular drink. Citrus twists and citrus spirals receive special mention here as they are a favourite little flourish, but with the more outlandish tropical concoctions let your imagination run riot — use as many skewered fruits, swizzle sticks and tiny parasols as you fancy!

Citrus twist Use a citrus peeler or very sharp knife to slice a thin, wide strip of peel from the citrus fruit, avoiding the bitter white pith. Make a small cut across the peel and twist it in opposite directions (do this over the drink to release a fine spray of zesty oils) and serve the twist on the side of the glass or in the drink.

Citrus spiral Use a citrus peeler, zester or sharp knife to slice a long, continuous strip of peel from the fruit. The longer the peel, the greater the curl.

for a special touch

Many recipes call for sugar syrup, which you can buy or very easily make. Simply place equal quantities of water and sugar in a saucepan and stir well to dissolve the sugar. Bring to the boil, reduce the heat and simmer until reduced by half. Allow to cool, pour into an airtight container and refrigerate.

Fruit purées give fruity cocktails that extra lift. All you do is blend fresh fruit with a fruit liqueur, pour it into a 500 ml (17 oz/2 cups) airtight container, seal and refrigerate. Try these! Mango Blend the flesh of 4 ripe mangoes with 60 ml (2 oz) mango liqueur.

Peach Blend 6–8 sliced peaches with 60 ml (2 oz) peach liqueur. Raspberry Blend two punnets of raspberries with 60 ml (2 oz) raspberry liqueur.

Strawberry Blend 500 g (1 lb 2 oz) of hulled strawberries with 60 ml (2 oz) strawberry liqueur.

Infused spirits have taken off in a big way. Vodka alone is now available in fantastic flavours such as bison grass, vanilla, honey, citrus, peach, blackcurrant, sloe berry, pepper and chocolate. But why not be your own mixmaster and infuse your own potions? Vodka is the perfect starting base as it is neutral in colour and flavour. Use good-quality vodka, start with small batches and plan ahead: you'll need to steep it for at least three days. The quantities here will infuse a 1 litre (35 oz) bottle of vodka, gin, vermouth or tequila, so adjust the ingredients accordingly. **Basil** or **mint** 8–10 basil or mint leaves, wrapped in a thin muslin cloth. **Blueberry** 15 blueberries. **Cinnamon** 2 cinnamon sticks. **Chilli** 5 red bird's eye chillies. **Coffee** 10–15 whole roasted coffee beans. **Lemon grass** 1–2 stems.

Lychee 8–10 peeled, seeded lychees — if tinned, add 30 ml (1 oz) lychee syrup. Peach 3 sliced peaches. Raspberry 15 raspberries. Strawberry 6 sliced strawberries. Vanilla 2 vanilla beans, sliced down the middle. Watermelon 10 nice chunks.

How to do it Pour your chosen spirit into a 1 litre (35 oz) airtight or screwcap container (reserve the empty bottle). Add the other ingredients, seal the lid tightly and store in a dark, cool, dry place for 3–5 days. Gently shake the mixture now and then and check how the flavour is developing. The longer you leave it, the stronger it will become. If it becomes too strong, dilute it with unflavoured spirits until you reach your preferred intensity. When you're done, strain the liquid into the original bottle and store in the freezer, ready to drink.

bubbles Nothing speaks of celebration, exhilaration, excitation and exaltation quite as eloquently as the popping of a Champagne cork and the gentle tinkle of clinking flutes. Champagne cocktails, fizzes,

sparkles and spritzers: all that whispers of laughter and joy is here in abundance to mark life's most precious moments. So bring out some icy cold bottles of your best bubbly stuff and get ready to shine!

Life isn't all beer and skittles — some occasions call for a dash of elegance and panache. And what could be more civilized and refined than sipping a Champagne cocktail while dressed to the nines and practising the gentle art of conversation in congenial company? The cocktails in this chapter are for special times — marriages, births, anniversaries — or whenever life's been a little flat and you need a fast injection of fun or exuberant decadence. But first to a point of protocol. Champagne refers to the much celebrated liquid produced in the French region of the same name, whose branding is zealously protected. Other bubblies made using the same technique are known by the more prosaic moniker of sparkling wine, but the end result is arguably equally delightful. Whether you imbibe Champagne or sparkling wine, these ambrosial cocktails deserve the best you can afford. And make sure you give your bubblies a really good chilling to bring out their luscious bouquet and mouthfeel. The cocktails in this chapter call on heavenly additions such as brandy; a cornucopia of fruits — orange, blackcurrant, blackberry, peach, pineapple and strawberry, as well as Limoncello — and classic spirits such as Campari and vodka. Other bar basics include mineral water, sugar, Angostura bitters and the odd bottle of pinot noir. So now that we've covered the essentials, let's get popping!

Fashions come and fashions go but the true classic
is untouchable.

classic champagne cocktail

1 sugar cube
dash of Angostura bitters
30 ml (1 oz) brandy
chilled Champagne or sparkling wine

Place the sugar cube in a chilled champagne flute. Add the bitters, then
the brandy. Slowly top up with Champagne or sparkling wine.

Serve these exquisite berry-laden bubbles on a silver platter in your finest flutes and wait for the accolades to roll in.

champagne berry cocktails

6 sugar cubes
dash of Angostura bitters
zest of 1 lime, very finely sliced
200 g (7 oz) blackberries, raspberries, blueberries or strawberries
1 bottle of chilled Champagne or sparkling wine

Place a cube of sugar in six chilled champagne flutes and add a dash of bitters to each. Divide the lime zest and berries among the flutes and slowly top up with Champagne or sparkling wine. Serves 6.

From sun-drenched lemon groves along the sparkling coast of Naples comes lovely Limoncello to make this cocktail shine.

limoncello cocktail

10 ml (¼ oz) lime juice
15 ml (½ oz) Limoncello
chilled Champagne or sparkling wine

Pour the lime juice and Limoncello into a chilled champagne flute, then slowly top up with Champagne or sparkling wine.

As opulent and lavish as the celebrated hotel that shares its name, this drink is all style.

savoy

15 ml (½ oz) Campari
15 ml (½ oz) ruby red grapefruit juice
15 ml (½ oz) lychee juice
chilled Champagne or sparkling wine
orange twist

Pour the Campari, grapefruit juice and lychee juice into a chilled champagne flute, then slowly top up with Champagne or sparkling wine. Garnish with a twist of orange.

savoy

Pining for a flirty encounter? Find a sexy stranger, flutter those lashes and sigh languorously as you nibble that cherry.

flirtini

15 ml (1/2 oz) pineapple vodka
15 ml (1/2 oz) pineapple juice
chilled Champagne or sparkling wine
maraschino cherry

Pour the vodka and pineapple juice into a chilled martini glass. Slowly top up with Champagne or sparkling wine and garnish with a maraschino cherry.

BARTENDER'S TIP Many vodka companies are now producing pineapple vodka, but if you can't find it you can use plain vodka.

If the original version isn't sinful enough, try this decadent crimson concoction.

scarlet bellini

15 ml (1/2 oz) peach liqueur
30 ml (1 oz) blood orange juice
chilled Champagne or sparkling wine
half a blood orange slice

Pour the peach liqueur and orange juice into a chilled champagne flute. Slowly top up with Champagne or sparkling wine. Garnish with half a slice of blood orange.

scarlet bellini

Adds colour to your cheeks and a little sparkle to your step.

cranberry and vodka sparkle

ice cubes
125 ml (4 oz/1/2 cup) cranberry juice
125 ml (4 oz/1/2 cup) lemonade or mineral water
10 ml (1/4 oz) lime juice
15 ml (1/2 oz) vodka

Half-fill a mixing jug with ice. Pour in the cranberry juice, lemonade or mineral water, lime juice and vodka. Stir, then pour into a highball glass.

Pucker up for a perky experience that kisses you right back.

blueberry sour

1 tablespoon frozen lemon sorbet
15 ml (1/2 oz) vodka
chilled Champagne or sparkling wine
6 blueberries

Spoon the sorbet into a chilled martini glass. Pour in the vodka and slowly top up with Champagne or sparkling wine. Garnish with blueberries.

blueberry sour

chic   If you feel sweetness is a plague and your wit and palate veer

sharply towards the dry side, you might find these elegant cocktails too

sexy for words. Oozing style and sophistication, these are drinks for

classy, confident types capable of taking the bitter with the sweet. Acerbic, astringent and invigorating aperitifs mix it with a dry, wry, macerating martinis to sharpen the mind as well as the appetite.

Gin, vodka and vermouth are the classic culprits behind this searingly smart set of seductive favourites and memorable martinis. Here our vodka takes on some ultra-cool associations, infused with bison grass and sloe berry. Campari makes a strong impression too. You'll find the odd liqueur from the more exotic end of the flavour spectrum: peach schnapps, contreau and vanilla liqueur. Japanese sake makes a surprise debut, emphasizing the cosmopolitan connections of this highly select company. A major bittersweet contributor to these bracing libations is a full-throttled squeeze of fresh citrus juice, from lemon and lime to ruby grapefruit with cranberry juice offering an equally tart rejoinder. Of course you'll need buckets of ice as these cocktails must be served arctically cold. And in keeping with our disapproval of ostentatious frippery, we shall also keep our garnishes simple and classy: olives, a twist of lemon or orange, a wedge of lime, the odd maraschino cherry and a lychee or two. Stock up on soda water, check your sugar syrup levels and maybe even invest in some lime juice cordial, by which we mean the syrupy, thick cordial extracted from real limes — and not the impossibly green cordial found on supermarket shelves! Over to you …

The perfect version of the perfect drink promises the perfect start to a perfect evening.

perfect martini

ice cubes
60 ml (2 oz) gin
15 ml (1/2 oz) dry vermouth
15 ml (1/2 oz) sweet vermouth
green olives or a lemon twist

Half-fill a mixing glass with ice. Pour in the gin, dry vermouth and sweet vermouth and stir. Strain into a chilled martini glass and garnish with green olives or a twist of lemon.

Not everyone can cope with a searingly dry martini. Here's one for those who appreciate the lusher side of life.

sweet martini

ice cubes
75 ml (2¹/2 oz) gin
15 ml (¹/2 oz) sweet red vermouth
maraschino cherry or an olive

Fill a mixing glass at least two-thirds full of ice. Add the gin and vermouth and stir gently. Strain into a chilled martini glass and garnish with a maraschino cherry or an olive.

perfect martini

Schoolgirl crushes are a thing of the past when the grown-up version tastes so much sweeter.

campari crush

crushed ice
30 ml (1 oz) gin
30 ml (1 oz) Campari
ruby red grapefruit juice
lime wedge

Fill a highball glass with crushed ice. Add the gin and Campari, then top up with grapefruit juice. Squeeze a lime wedge into the glass and add the squeezed wedge to the drink.

You either love it or hate it, but the bitterly complex negroni
has legion fans, having graced menus for close to a century.

negroni

ice cubes
30 ml (1 oz) gin
30 ml (1 oz) sweet vermouth
30 ml (1 oz) Campari
soda water (optional)
orange twist

Half-fill a mixing glass with ice. Add the gin, vermouth and Campari. Stir
well, then strain into a chilled cocktail glass. Add a dash of soda water if
you wish. Garnish with a twist of orange.

campari crush

Check the current, set your sails and let the ocean winds take you where they will.

seabreeze

ice cubes
45 ml (1¹/₂ oz) vodka
60 ml (2 oz) cranberry juice
60 ml (2 oz) ruby red grapefruit juice
15 ml (¹/₂ oz) lime juice
lime twist

Half-fill a cocktail shaker with ice. Add the vodka, cranberry juice, grapefruit juice and lime juice. Shake well and strain into a highball glass half-filled with ice. Garnish with a twist of lime.

Amble through this cocktail as you would a rambling orchard on a clear, sunny day.

life's good

ice cubes
45 ml (1 1/2 oz) sloe berry vodka
15 ml (1/2 oz) lychee juice
15 ml (1/2 oz) cranberry juice
15 ml (1/2 oz) strawberry purée (see recipe on page 23)
lime wedge

Half-fill a cocktail shaker with ice. Add the vodka, lychee juice, cranberry juice and strawberry purée. Shake vigorously and strain into a chilled martini glass. Squeeze the lime wedge over the drink and add it as a garnish.

BARTENDER'S TIP For an after-dinner drink, sprinkle with grated chocolate.

life's good

Bison grass has reputed aphrodisiac qualities — for buffaloes at least. Who knows what a shot or two might do for you?

bison kick

ice cubes
45 ml (1½ oz) bison grass vodka
10 ml (¼ oz) sake
30 ml (1 oz) watermelon juice
15 ml (½ oz) lychee juice
10 ml (¼ oz) sugar syrup
1 peeled fresh lychee

Half-fill a cocktail shaker with ice. Add the vodka, sake, watermelon juice, lychee juice and sugar syrup. Shake vigorously and strain into a chilled cocktail glass. Garnish with a lychee.

Crank up your courage, release the throttle and go down in a blaze of glory.

kamikaze

ice cubes
45 ml (1 1/2 oz) vodka
15 ml (1/2 oz) Cointreau
30 ml (1 oz) lemon juice
dash of lime juice cordial

Half-fill a cocktail shaker with ice. Add the vodka, Cointreau, lemon juice and lime juice cordial. Shake well and strain into a chilled cocktail glass. Garnish with a cocktail umbrella.

bison kick

Woo! Woo! Chattanooga here we come! A few of these down your gullet and you'll be flying along.

WOO WOO

ice cubes
lime wedge
60 ml (2 oz) vodka
15 ml (½ oz) peach schnapps
cranberry juice

Half-fill a cocktail shaker with ice. Squeeze the lime wedge into the shaker, then add the vodka and peach schnapps. Shake, then strain into an old-fashioned glass half-filled with ice. Add the squeezed lime wedge and top up with cranberry juice.

The blueberry of happiness brightens up old Tom's club lounge classic.

berry collins

2 tablespoons blueberries
15 ml (1/2 oz) sugar syrup
ice cubes
45 ml (11/2 oz) gin
30 ml (1 oz) vanilla liqueur
15 ml (1/2 oz) lemon juice
cranberry juice or lemonade

Muddle the blueberries with the sugar syrup in a cocktail shaker. Add a scoop of ice, then the gin, vanilla liqueur and lemon juice. Shake vigorously and pour into a tall glass to 2.5 cm (1 inch) from the top, then top up with cranberry juice or lemonade.

berry collins

jungle juice Forget the concrete jungle, we're off to the rum jungle on a high-spirited cocktail safari, so grab your pith helmet and insect repellent and get ready for some wild nights, no passouts allowed. Just

remember jungle potions have potent effects — imbibe too many and you might start seeing blue devils and pink elephants. Now turn the music up a notch, it's time to jungle boogie! Get down, get down …

This is a story about rambunctious rum runners, punch-happy persuaders, cool customers from the Caribbean and their Mexican mates — a gang of heavy-duty party troopers who know how to get things started! Their fiery, fruity prescriptions will rev up the action at the drop of a hat and inspire bouts of revelry and even devilry. Essential supplies for this bacchanalian adventure include rum aplenty, from standard to overproof intensity. Procure several bottles of tequila and a generous supply of gin and vodka. A few heady punches call for ingredients such as bubbly, Pimm's No. 1, red wine, bourbon and sweet vermouth. It's bound to get hot so keep buckets of ice on hand, as well as thirst quenchers such as cola and lemonade. Deep in the jungle pluck a fresh harvest of limes, lemons and oranges to squeeze into your drinks (you'll need your vitamin C). Other reviving essences include fruity liquers, Galliano and the darkly mysterious Kahlúa. Blue curaçao, green Chartreuse, green crème de menthe and grenadine are the secret to the exquisite bird-of-paradise colours glimpsed in our potions, the likes of which are rarely seen. So let our journey begin.

Family celebrations call for a certain calibre of drink.

Here's something that will keep everybody happy.

pimm's punch

375 ml (13 oz/1½ cups)
  orange juice
ice cubes
400 ml (14 oz) Pimm's No. 1
400 ml (14 oz) bourbon

185 ml (6 oz) sweet vermouth
185 ml (6 oz) white rum
1 bottle of Champagne or
  sparkling wine
3 cups chopped fresh fruit

Freeze 90 ml (3 oz) of the orange juice in an ice-cube tray. Half-fill a punch bowl with ice, then add the Pimm's, bourbon, vermouth, rum, remaining orange juice and the Champagne or sparkling wine. Stir in the fresh fruit and the frozen orange juice ice cubes. Serves 10.

BARTENDER'S TIP Some people like to add mint leaves and cucumber slices.

While away a lazy afternoon with a good pal and a jug of fruity sangria.

sangria

15 ml (1/2 oz) lemon juice	45 ml (11/2 oz) gin
15 ml (1/2 oz) orange juice	45 ml (11/2 oz) vodka
11/2 tablespoons caster (superfine) sugar	1 lemon
1 bottle of red wine	1 orange
570 ml (20 oz) lemonade	1 lime
	ice cubes

Put the lemon juice, orange juice and sugar in a large jug or bowl and stir until the sugar has dissolved. Add the red wine, lemonade, gin and vodka. Cut the lemon, orange and lime in half, remove the seeds and slice finely. Add the fruit to the jug, fill with ice, stir and serve. Serves 10.

pimm's punch

Exquisitely refreshing, this Caribbean classic is excellent for the constitution as well as the conversation.

bacardi cocktail

ice cubes
60 ml (2 oz) white Bacardi rum
30 ml (1 oz) lemon or lime juice
10 ml (¼ oz) grenadine
maraschino cherry

Half-fill a cocktail shaker with ice. Add the Bacardi, lemon or lime juice and grenadine, then shake well and strain into a chilled cocktail glass. Garnish with a maraschino cherry.

Throw off the shackles, free your mind and embrace the spirit of revolution.

cuba libre

ice cubes
60 ml (2 oz) white rum
6 lime wedges
cola
lime wedge

Half-fill a highball glass with ice. Add the rum, squeeze the lime wedges into the glass, then add the squeezed wedges to the drink. Top up with cola and garnish with a wedge of lime.

cuba libre

It's a brave babe who waves the red flag but several of these should steel your nerve.

brave bull

ice cubes
30 ml (1 oz) Kahlúa
45 ml (1½ oz) tequila

Half-fill an old-fashioned glass with ice. Add the Kahlúa, then add the tequila. Swirl gently before drinking.

South of the border the party starts early and finishes late.

Celebrate with a local shout.

olé

ice cubes
45 ml (1 1/2 oz) tequila
30 ml (1 oz) banana liqueur
dash of blue curaçao

Half-fill a cocktail shaker with ice. Add the tequila and banana liqueur, then shake well. Strain into a small, chilled cocktail glass. Tip a dash of blue curaçao into the drink to achieve a two-tone effect.

olé

Whatever you do, don't try to order another one of these after you've finished the first.

freddie fudpucker

ice cubes
45 ml (1 1/2 oz) tequila
15 ml (1/2 oz) Galliano
60 ml (2 oz) orange juice
half an orange slice
maraschino cherry

Half-fill a cocktail shaker with ice. Add the tequila, Galliano and orange juice, shake vigorously and strain into a chilled cocktail glass. Garnish with half a slice of orange and a maraschino cherry.

Whatever issues Harvey may have had with that wall,
it certainly resulted in a classic drop.

harvey wallbanger

crushed ice
30 ml (1 oz) vodka
10 ml (¼ oz) Galliano
orange juice
half an orange slice

Half-fill a highball glass with crushed ice. Add the vodka and Galliano,
then top up with orange juice. Garnish with half a slice of orange.

harvey wallbanger

frou frou Frills and thrills galore for those fancying a little afternoon delight or a fleeting flirtation with sweetness and light. From the decadently opulent to the wildly whimsical, nothing here is to be taken

too seriously. It's high time to flaunt it so frock up for a full-on fanfare.

Flounce about in your flashiest feathers, primp and preen your prettiest

peacock plumes and settle back for a fantasia on ice.

This chapter could almost be described as a midsummer night's dream. So let us introduce a tutti-frutti cast of players whose sole mission is to entice the senses and tickle the most fantastical of fancies — to utterly delight, indulge and entertain. What follows is a kaleidoscope of technicolour dreams featuring a vast, eclectic troop of royal luminaries such as Champagne, Cointreau, Pernod and Parfait Amour, cameo appearances by instantly recognizable types such as gin and white rum (clearly low-lifes!), a gamut of resplendent liquers — an ensemble supported by notables such as amaretto, Sambuca, Malibu and blue curaçao. Keeping up appearances is integral to the show, with many a flamboyant flourish anticipated from exotic fruits; expect juicy performances and an acerbic wit from lemons, limes and pineapples. Plot thickeners include agents as diverse as Angostura bitters, sugar syrup and raspberry cordial and lemonade. And for comic relief, don't miss a rib-tickling appearance by a liquorice allsort and a jelly bean! All in all, a glittering show at once zany, capricious and wanton, guaranteed to make you feel for one tizzy, giddy moment gloriously and unashamedly *chi chi*. So let the show begin …

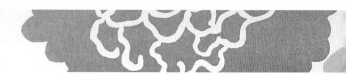

Make like the bright young things of the Roaring Twenties and dazzle the boys with this snappy number.

strawberry flapper

4 hulled strawberries
4 ice cubes
15 ml (1/2 oz) strawberry liqueur
chilled Champagne or sparkling wine

Place the strawberries, ice cubes and strawberry liqueur in a heavy-duty blender, then blend until smooth. Pour into a chilled champagne flute and slowly top up with Champagne or sparkling wine.

This magical version of a childhood classic could have slipped straight out of *Alice in Wonderland*.

raspberry champagne spider

1–2 raspberry sorbet balls
chilled Champagne or sparkling wine

Place one or two balls of raspberry sorbet in a chilled champagne flute and slowly top up with Champagne or sparkling wine.

BARTENDER'S TIP Scoop a tub of raspberry sorbet into small balls with a melon baller and freeze until needed.

raspberry champagne spider

Candy sweet and cute as a button — just remember this one
is *not* for the kiddies!

jelly bean

ice cubes
15 ml (1/2 oz) Sambuca
10 ml (1/4 oz) raspberry cordial
lemonade
jelly beans

Fill a cocktail glass with ice. Add the Sambuca and raspberry cordial, then
top up with lemonade. Garnish with jelly beans.

It takes all sorts to make the world go round, but not too many to set it spinning!

liquorice allsort

ice cubes
15 ml (1/2 oz) black Sambuca
15 ml (1/2 oz) strawberry liqueur
15 ml (1/2 oz) Malibu
60 ml (2 oz) cream
liquorice allsort or multi-coloured confectionery

Half-fill a cocktail shaker with ice. Add the Sambuca, strawberry liqueur, Malibu and cream and shake well. Strain into a chilled cocktail glass and garnish with a liquorice allsort or other confectionery on the rim.

No-one will ever blow raspberries at this bloomin' beautiful extravaganza.

red blossom

ice cubes
45 ml (1¹/2 oz) gin
15 ml (¹/2 oz) peach liqueur
2 tablespoons raspberries
15 ml (¹/2 oz) lemon juice
15 ml (¹/2 oz) sugar syrup
3 blueberries

Add a scoop of ice to a cocktail shaker, then the gin, peach liqueur, raspberries, lemon juice and sugar syrup. Shake vigorously and strain into a chilled martini glass. Garnish with blueberries.

Love, sweet love, can so easily turn sour, but this old faithful will never let you down.

per f'amour

ice cubes
15 ml (1/2 oz) Cointreau
15 ml (1/2 oz) Parfait Amour
45 ml (11/2 oz) orange juice
dash of egg white
orange twist

Half-fill a cocktail shaker with ice. Add the Cointreau, Parfait Amour, orange juice and a dash of egg white. Shake well until frothy, then strain into a chilled martini glass. Garnish with a twist of orange.

red blossom

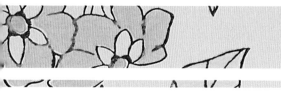

Recommended for internal use only, this frothy formulation is guaranteed to leave no tears.

shampoo

15 ml (1/2 oz) gin
15 ml (1/2 oz) lemon juice
dash of Pernod
dash of blue curaçao
chilled Champagne or sparkling wine
lemon twist

Pour the gin, then the lemon juice, Pernod and blue curaçao into a chilled champagne flute. Slowly top up with Champagne or sparkling wine and garnish with a twist of lemon.

When the green-eyed monster strikes, give the savage beast a
dose of its own medicine.

envy

ice cubes
15 ml (1/2 oz) white rum
15 ml (1/2 oz) amaretto
15 ml (1/2 oz) blue curaçao
15 ml (1/2 oz) lime juice
80 ml (21/2 oz) pineapple juice
pineapple wedge

Half-fill a cocktail shaker with ice. Add the rum, amaretto, blue curaçao,
lime juice and pineapple juice. Shake well, then strain into a highball glass
half-filled with ice. Garnish with a wedge of pineapple.

shampoo

tropicana Imagine yourself in an equatorial loveland sequestered from care, sipping like a giant hummingbird on precious nectars extracted from the rampant fruits of the warm wet earth. Wear a flower in your

hair and feel the sensual island breeze caress your sun-kissed cheeks. Marvel at the mighty sun's slow trajectory through the sky and at its fiery demise. This is the island time forgot. Welcome to paradise.

When the antics of this maddening world start to drive you bananas and make you lose your coconuts, you know you need to pack up your bongos and go troppo for a while. Extract yourself from the feverish melée and tune into island time, where life has a slower, stronger pulse and moves at a leisurely pace. Feel the slow crash of the surf on the beach, dig your toes deep into fine white squeaky-clean sand and then administer some strong tropical medicines such as rum in the form of a daiquiri or piña colada. For the full island experience, don't forget the Grand Marnier, Galliano, Malibu, and don't skimp on the cream, the milk or the coconut cream. The pounding sun and soaring mercury can challenge the equanimity, but mercifully this is an abundant place, where fruits and berries grow in jungly profusion to slake your thirst and keep you cool. Celebrate nature's bounty with fruity liquers and purées in a rainbow of flavours. Even our 'dear little water' vodka is infused with luscious essences — citrus, vanilla and currants. Other essential requirements in this magical place are a cargo hold of cold, cold ice, cocktail umbrellas, a deckchair, sarong (or a grass skirt if you prefer), an outlandish pair of sunglasses, a flouncy broad-rimmed hat and a nice pair of lovely hands to rub some sunscreen into those out of the way spots. Aloha, heaven.

A tempting taste of paradise in every tiny shot.

passionfruit and vanilla vodka jelly shots

1 gelatine leaf
15 ml (1/2 oz) sugar syrup
80 ml (21/2 oz) passionfruit pulp
80 ml (21/2 oz) vanilla vodka

Soak the gelatine leaf in cold water. Heat the sugar syrup and passionfruit pulp until just hot. Squeeze the liquid out of the gelatine, add the gelatine to the passionfruit mixture and stir to dissolve. Cool, stir in the vodka and pour into six shot glasses. Refrigerate for 3 hours, or until set. Makes 6.

Listen to the calypso rhythms in your mind, jump into the nearest banana boat and find your island in the sun.

banana daiquiri

half a banana, peeled
30 ml (1 oz) white rum
15 ml (1/2 oz) banana liqueur
15 ml (1/2 oz) lime juice
15 ml (1/2 oz) sugar syrup
1 cup crushed ice
banana slice, dipped in lemon juice

Place the banana, rum, banana liqueur, lime juice and sugar syrup in a blender and blend until smooth. Add the crushed ice and blend until the mixture is the consistency of shaved ice. Pour into a chilled cocktail glass and garnish with a slice of banana.

passionfruit and vanilla vodka jelly shots

Any time you want to impress the pants off somebody
wow them with this awesomely mesmerizing margarita.

blood orange margarita

egg white
caster (superfine) sugar
ice cubes
45 ml (1 1/2 oz) gold tequila
15 ml (1/2 oz) mandarin liqueur
   or Grand Marnier

15 ml (1/2 oz) lime juice
30 ml (1 oz) blood orange juice
10 ml (1/4 oz) sugar syrup

Dip the rim of a cocktail glass in a saucer of egg white, then a saucer of sugar, shaking off any excess. Chill. Add a scoop of ice to a cocktail shaker, then the tequila, mandarin liqueur or Grand Marnier, lime juice, blood orange juice and sugar syrup. Shake vigorously and strain into the sugar-frosted cocktail glass.

When the temperature starts getting hellishly hot, here's a diabolically refreshing diversion for blasted palates.

diablo

ice cubes
45 ml (1¹/2 oz) currant vodka
30 ml (1 oz) blackberry liqueur
30 ml (1 oz) pineapple juice
pineapple leaf

Add a scoop of ice to a cocktail shaker, then the vodka, blackberry liqueur and pineapple juice. Shake vigorously and strain into a chilled martini glass. Garnish with a pineapple leaf.

diablo

No sand, no insects, no seaweed. This has to be better than the real thing!

sex on the beach

ice cubes
45 ml (1¹/2 oz) vodka
15 ml (¹/2 oz) peach schnapps
45 ml (1¹/2 oz) pineapple juice
45 ml (1¹/2 oz) cranberry juice
crushed ice

Half-fill a cocktail shaker with ice. Add the vodka, schnapps, pineapple juice and cranberry juice and shake well. Strain into a tall cocktail glass half-filled with crushed ice.

When nothing else is quite as it seems, rest assured this fruity fantasy has nothing to hide.

masquerade

ice cubes
45 ml (1½ oz) citrus vodka
15 ml (½ oz) apple schnapps
30 ml (1 oz) watermelon juice
15 ml (½ oz) apple juice
dash of lime juice
thin apple slices

Half-fill a cocktail shaker with ice. Add the vodka, schnapps, watermelon juice, apple juice and a dash of lime juice. Shake vigorously and strain into a chilled martini glass. Garnish with thin slices of apple.

masquerade

The tango requires passion, style and coordination so it's probably a good idea to dance first, drink later.

mango tango

15 ml (1/2 oz) mango liqueur
15 ml (1/2 oz) Grand Marnier
15 ml (1/2 oz) sugar syrup
15 ml (1/2 oz) cream
15 ml (1/2 oz) milk
half a mango, peeled and diced
8 ice cubes
mango purée (see recipe on page 23)

Place the mango liqueur, Grand Marnier, sugar syrup, cream, milk, mango and ice in a heavy-duty blender and blend until thick and smooth. Pour into a tall, chilled cocktail glass and garnish with a swirl of fresh mango purée.

This really should be drunk out of a hollowed-out pineapple, and preferably in the shallow end of a pool!

piña colada

1 cup crushed ice
45 ml (1¹/2 oz) white rum
15 ml (¹/2 oz) coconut cream
15 ml (¹/2 oz) Malibu
100 ml (3¹/2 oz) pineapple juice
15 ml (¹/2 oz) sugar syrup
pineapple leaves

Place the crushed ice, rum, coconut cream, Malibu, pineapple juice and sugar syrup in a blender and blend until the mixture is the consistency of shaved ice. Pour into a large, chilled cocktail glass and garnish with pineapple leaves and a cocktail umbrella.

It's easy to get spliced on this wondrous pine–melon fusion.

It can happen in a trice.

splice

crushed ice
15 ml (1/2 oz) melon liqueur
15 ml (1/2 oz) Cointreau
15 ml (1/2 oz) Malibu
100 ml (31/2 oz) pineapple juice
60 ml (2 oz) cream
pineapple wedge
melon ball

Place some crushed ice, melon liqueur, Cointreau, Malibu, pineapple juice
and cream in a blender and blend well. Pour into a large, chilled goblet.
Garnish with a wedge of pineapple and a melon ball. Serve with a straw.

San Tropez is so very far from here, but with this chic number

a Riviera moment is just a swizzle stick away.

chi chi

crushed ice
45 ml (1 1/2 oz) vodka
15 ml (1/2 oz) Malibu
15 ml (1/2 oz) coconut cream
125 ml (4 oz/1/2 cup) pineapple juice
pineapple wedge
strawberry slices

Place some crushed ice, vodka, Malibu, coconut cream and pineapple juice in a blender and blend well. Pour into a large, chilled tumbler and garnish with a small wedge of pineapple and strawberry slices.

muddled It isn't always such a bad thing to feel a little muddled. Indeed, a muddled cocktail is a wonderful thing! The drinks in this chapter draw their inspiration from exotic corners of the globe, seeking

out wild combinations of delirious new flavours to baffle the tongue, awaken the tastebuds and send your senses spinning. It's only natural to feel a little disoriented. Follow your nose and you'll be fine …

It all began innocently enough, as excellent adventures often do. Someone muddled and mashed and ground and gently bashed some fruit and herbs around in a cocktail shaker, releasing a burst of powerfully fresh flavours into our tired old drinks, instantly firing up our fatigued palates. Suddenly we were bounding about in Chile or was it Peru, sampling copious amounts of pisco, a clear, brandy-like spirit that both countries claim as their national drink. Who are we to argue? Next stop Brazil, where we took on board some cachaça, a sterling distillation of unrefined sugarcane juice roughly translating as 'farmer's drink'. But it was only when somebody muddled some kiwifruit and ginger into their caipiroska that things started getting really confusing! Sometime around sunset we meandered down Mexico way to sample a little gold tequila, simultaneously stumbling upon some wondrous new tequilas spiked with vanilla and chilli! After our feisty , fiery latino lovers we happily surrendered to wildly wonderful vodkas tasting of peach, passionfruit, raspberries, blueberries, strawberries, lemon grass, cinnamon and honey and flavours crushed from citrus and blood orange. Where we are now, nobody knows, but life will never be the same again.

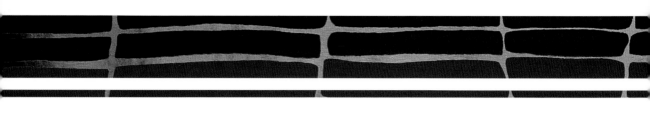

A caipirinha made from vodka rather than cachaça. Boy, those Brazilians sure know how to create a carnival atmosphere!

caipiroska

1 lime, chopped
3 teaspoons caster (superfine) sugar
15 ml (½ oz) sugar syrup
ice cubes
60 ml (2 oz) vodka

Muddle the lime with the sugar and sugar syrup in a cocktail shaker. Add a scoop of ice and the vodka. Shake vigorously and strain into a chilled tumbler.

BARTENDER'S TIP You could make a minty caipiroska by muddling eight mint leaves with the limes, sugar and sugar syrup.

The vibrant flavours in this lively number will make your tongue do a capoeira and your body bossa nova!

kiwi and ginger caipiroska

1 kiwifruit, peeled
half a lime, chopped
1 teaspoon caster (superfine) sugar
ice cubes
45 ml (1½ oz) honey vodka
15 ml (½ oz) ginger liqueur

Muddle the kiwifruit and lime with the sugar in a cocktail shaker. Add a scoop of ice, then the vodka and ginger liqueur. Shake vigorously and strain into a chilled tumbler.

BARTENDER'S TIP Honey vodka is commercially available but if your liquor store can't supply it, replace it with plain vodka.

caipiroska

The sparkling riches gleaming within may prove irresistibly alluring. Get out your shovel and start digging.

acapulco gold

1 lemon, chopped
15 ml (1/2 oz) sugar syrup
ice cubes
45 ml (11/2 oz) chilli-infused tequila (see recipe on page 24)
15 ml (1/2 oz) vanilla liqueur
lemonade

Muddle the lemon and sugar syrup in a cocktail shaker. Add a scoop of ice, then the tequila and vanilla liqueur. Shake vigorously and strain into a tall, chilled glass 2.5 cm (1 inch) from the top, then top up with lemonade.

When lambada rhythms start to play, slurp, suck or lick one of these and start to sway.

lambada lick

half a peach, chopped
30 ml (1 oz) passionfruit purée
15 ml (1/2 oz) sugar syrup
ice cubes
45 ml (1 1/2 oz) cachaça
dash of lime juice

Muddle the peach and passionfruit purée with the sugar syrup in a cocktail shaker. Add a scoop of ice, then the cachaça and lime juice. Shake vigorously and strain into a chilled tumbler.

acapulco gold

Destined to stir the passions of any hot-blooded woman.

señorita

1 tablespoon raspberries
1 tablespoon blueberries
15 ml (½ oz) sugar syrup
ice cubes
45 ml (1½ oz) gold tequila
15 ml (½ oz) raspberry liqueur
30 ml (1 oz) cranberry juice
lime wedge

Muddle the raspberries and blueberries with the sugar syrup in a cocktail shaker. Add a scoop of ice, then the tequila and raspberry liqueur. Shake vigorously and strain into a chilled tumbler 2.5 cm (1 inch) from the top, then top up with cranberry juice. Garnish with a wedge of lime.

Will bring even the proudest man to his knees.

el hombre

half a lemon, chopped
30 ml (1 oz) peach purée (see recipe on page 23)
15 ml (1/2 oz) sugar syrup
ice cubes
45 ml (11/2 oz) vanilla-infused tequila (see recipe on page 25)
15 ml (1/2 oz) peach liqueur

Muddle the lemon and peach purée with the sugar syrup in a cocktail shaker. Add a scoop of ice, then the tequila and peach liqueur. Shake vigorously and strain into a chilled tumbler.

señorita

To witness a blood sunset in all its glory can be a rather intoxicating experience.

blood sunset

3 strawberries, halved
half a blood orange, chopped
15 ml (1/2 oz) sugar syrup
ice cubes
45 ml (11/2 oz) vodka
dash of lime juice

Muddle the strawberries and blood orange with the sugar syrup in a cocktail shaker. Add a scoop of ice, then the vodka and lime juice. Shake vigorously and pour into a chilled tumbler.

Jump into your zaniest costume and you'll really start to dig this outlandishly colourful outfit.

zoot suit

half an orange, chopped
half a lime, chopped
15 ml (1/2 oz) sugar syrup
ice cubes
45 ml (11/2 oz) Campari
30 ml (1 oz) blood orange juice

Muddle the orange and lime with the sugar syrup in a cocktail shaker. Add a scoop of ice, then the Campari and blood orange juice. Shake vigorously and strain into a chilled tumbler.

zoot suit

club lounge After a long, hard day spent engaged in strictly masculine pursuits, it was customary for men of good breeding to unwind in the rarefied ambience of the nineteenth hole, otherwise

known as the gentleman's bar. In this world away from women, the man about town was free to indulge in a little dignified swilling of a clutch of classic drinks. All good sport, really. Who could blame them?

Stake your place on a dark leather chesterfield and sink down into a boys' own world where topics of great import and jocularity are mulled over at leisure, tall tales are traded and deals are done over a card game and a drink or three. Settle back as the shadows lengthen from late in the afternoon until deep into the evening. Perhaps Sir would care to begin with a few afternoon refreshments, a sundowner or an appetite-provoking aperitif? We venture to suggest Sir might also wish to sample some appealing classics mixed from gin and vodka, or perhaps some relaxing brandy-based drinks, or if Sir has had a very rugged day he might prefer to proceed directly to our straight talkin', sharp shootin', hard-hitting, no-nonsense types such as whisky or bourbon. And when the business of the day is done, Sir may wish to sample a little snifter of late-night, top-shelf liqueurs such as cognac, Drambuie and Bénédictine. A word to the bar manager: invest in some Cointreau and vermouth, stock up on lemon, lime, orange and tomato juice and mixers such as soda water, ginger ale and cola, and check your supply of bitters, lime juice cordial, grenadine and sugar syrup. Naturally, our garnishes are free of feminizing influences: a maraschino cherry is as fancy as it gets, but the usual adornments are slices of lime, lemon, orange or a sprig of mint. Remember, discretion is the key …

Steel your resolve and face the world with a gimlet eye.
At the very least you'll ward off scurvy.

gimlet

ice cubes
45 ml (1 1/2 oz) gin
15 ml (1/2 oz) lime juice
15 ml (1/2 oz) lime juice cordial
lime twist
lime wedge

Half-fill a mixing glass with ice. Add the gin, lime juice and lime juice cordial and stir well. Strain into a chilled goblet and garnish with a twist of lime and a wedge of lime.

Those spirited old sailors of the high seas knew full well
not to go overboard on lime rickeys.

lime rickey

ice cubes
45 ml (1 1/2 oz) gin
15 ml (1/2 oz) sugar syrup
15 ml (1/2 oz) lime juice
dash of Angostura bitters
soda water
lime twist
lime slice

Half-fill a highball glass with ice. Add the gin, sugar syrup, lime juice and
a dash of bitters, then top up with soda water. Garnish with a twist of
lime and a slice of lime.

gimlet

A classy beverage, but not for high tea. Just remember, one is a potent social lubricant, two will knock you off your trolley.

long island iced tea

ice cubes
15 ml (1/2 oz) white rum
15 ml (1/2 oz) vodka
15 ml (1/2 oz) gin
15 ml (1/2 oz) Cointreau
15 ml (1/2 oz) tequila
1/2 teaspoon lime juice
cola
lime wedge

Half-fill a highball glass with ice. Add the rum, vodka, gin, Cointreau, tequila and lime juice, then top up with cola. Stir well with a swizzle stick and garnish with a wedge of lime.

After a long, hot and sultry day, here's something tall, cool and soothing to settle your sulky southern belle.

mint julep

ice cubes
60 ml (2 oz) bourbon
8 mint leaves
15 ml (1/2 oz) sugar syrup
dash of dark rum or brandy
mint sprig

Half-fill a mixing glass with ice. Add the bourbon, mint and sugar, then stir. Strain into a highball glass filled with ice and stir gently until the glass becomes frosted. Top with a dash of rum or brandy. Garnish with a sprig of mint and serve with a long straw.

BARTENDER'S TIP Some people like to add a few chunks of cucumber for extra refreshment.

mint julep

Slow down sonny, pull up a chair, linger awhile and reflect on days gone by.

old fashioned

1 sugar cube
dash of Angostura bitters
soda water
ice cubes
60 ml (2 oz) bourbon
orange twist (optional)

Place the sugar cube in an old-fashioned glass. Add the bitters and let it soak into the sugar. Add a splash of soda water and enough ice to half-fill the glass. Pour in the bourbon and stir to dissolve the sugar. Garnish with a twist of orange if you wish.

Whether you want to get high or just have a ball, this drink lives up to its name.

highball

ice cubes
45 ml (1½ oz) rye whiskey
soda water or ginger ale
lemon twist

Half-fill a highball glass with ice. Add the whiskey and top up with soda water or ginger ale. Garnish with a twist of lemon.

old fashioned

There's nothing quite like a brisk tumbler in the rye.

whiskey sour

ice cubes
45 ml (1 1/2 oz) rye whiskey
15 ml (1/2 oz) Cointreau
15 ml (1/2 oz) lemon juice
15 ml (1/2 oz) sugar syrup
maraschino cherry

Half-fill a cocktail shaker with ice. Add the whiskey, Cointreau, lemon juice and sugar syrup, then shake well. Strain into a tumbler and garnish with a maraschino cherry.

For a brave, brave heart, slip a few under your kilt.

rob roy

ice cubes
60 ml (2 oz) Scotch whisky
30 ml (1 oz) sweet red vermouth
dash of Angostura bitters
maraschino cherry

Half-fill a cocktail shaker with ice. Add the whisky, vermouth and bitters, then shake well. Strain into a chilled cocktail glass and garnish with a maraschino cherry.

mellow   Creamy, milky, sweet and dreamy, these cocktails are surely sent from high above to melt away the cares of the mortal day. At the end of a meal, these mellifluous offerings are like manna from heaven,

delivering to all good people their just desserts, radiating smiles of deep contentment and a warm inner glow. Soothing and sublime, they are the supreme indulgence. Go on, you *know* you want to …

This chapter has special meaning for people who are blessed with a pronounced predilection for creamy concoctions infused with sugar and spice and **all things nice**. This is the chapter where liquers are in their element, where Heaven meets Earth, and angels sing high up in the firmament (you might need to sip a few liqueurs to hear them). The word 'liqueur' derives from the Latin meaning to melt, or to dissolve — a very accurate description of their **mellowing effects** upon the human body. Liqueurs have been around for centuries and are now available in every conceivable flavour from fruity and herbal through to **coffee** and chocolatey. Just as well really. And while they can be combined in innumerable ways, the ones you'll find keep cropping up in the most popular of our mellow cocktails include Irish cream, **Frangelico**, Cointreau, **Galliano**, Tia Maria, Kahlúa, **chocolate liqueur**, advocaat and crème de cacao. Which is not to say you have to buy them all to be the consummate host — but then again, who's to stop you? Other valued friends from the spirit world that make their influence keenly felt here include gin, vodka and **brandy**, with special dispensation given to **indulge** in chocolate syrup, **cream**, honey and crushed hazelnuts. Why delay, life is short!

Frankly, my dear, after several of these you certainly will not give a damn.

frankie

ice cubes
15 ml (1/2 oz) Frangelico
15 ml (1/2 oz) Kahlúa
30 ml (1 oz) Irish cream
30 ml (1 oz) cream
very finely crushed hazelnuts

Half-fill a cocktail shaker with ice. Add the Frangelico, Kahlúa, Irish cream and cream. Shake vigorously, then strain into a large chilled cocktail glass. Serve sprinkled with very finely crushed hazelnuts.

Sometimes comfort is the order of the day. Let this fluffy favourite unruffle your feathers and smooth away your troubles.

fluffy duck

ice cubes
15 ml (1/2 oz) advocaat
15 ml (1/2 oz) gin
15 ml (1/2 oz) Cointreau
30 ml (1 oz) orange juice
30 ml (1 oz) cream
lemonade

Half-fill a highball glass with ice. Add the advocaat, gin, Cointreau, orange juice and cream, then top up with lemonade.

frankie

Keep reminding yourself, this is *not* a chocolate milkshake.

toblerone

1 teaspoon honey
15 ml (1/2 oz) chocolate syrup
finely chopped hazelnuts
ice cubes
15 ml (1/2 oz) Frangelico
15 ml (1/2 oz) Irish cream

15 ml (1/2 oz) Tia Maria
15 ml (1/2 oz) creamy chocolate
  liqueur
60 ml (2 oz) cream
shaved chocolate

Drizzle the honey and a teaspoon of the chocolate syrup into a large chilled martini glass. Sprinkle with chopped hazelnuts and chill. Half-fill a cocktail shaker with ice. Pour in the Frangelico, Irish cream, Tia Maria, chocolate liqueur and cream and shake well. Strain into the chilled martini glass and garnish with shaved chocolate.

A chocolate martini! Are we in heaven yet girls?

chocotini

50 g (1³/4 oz) chocolate
ice cubes
60 ml (2 oz) vodka
30 ml (1 oz) brown crème de cacao

Melt the chocolate in a heatproof bowl over simmering water. Dip the rim of a martini glass in the chocolate, or dot the chocolate around the rim. Chill the glass. Half-fill a cocktail shaker with ice. Add the vodka and crème de cacao, shake vigorously and strain into the chilled martini glass.

chocotini

A nightcap to give any budding romance a blooming chance.

caramel bud

ice cubes
15 ml (1/2 oz) butterscotch schnapps
30 ml (1 oz) chocolate liqueur
15 ml (1/2 oz) white crème de cacao
30 ml (1 oz) cream
grated chocolate

Half-fill a cocktail shaker with ice. Add the butterscotch schnapps, chocolate liqueur, crème de cacao and cream. Shake vigorously and strain into a chilled cocktail glass. Garnish with grated chocolate.

Sheer luxury! Why wear anything else?

silk stocking

ice cubes
15 ml (1/2 oz) butterscotch schnapps
15 ml (1/2 oz) advocaat
30 ml (1 oz) white crème de cacao
30 ml (1 oz) cream
white chocolate shards

Half-fill a cocktail shaker with ice. Add the butterscotch schnapps, advocaat, crème de cacao and cream. Shake vigorously and strain into a chilled martini glass. Garnish with shards of white chocolate.

silk stocking

Settle back, sink down and stretch those legs out. It's time for some seriously smooth cruising.

golden cadillac

ice cubes
30 ml (1 oz) Galliano
30 ml (1 oz) white crème de cacao
30 ml (1 oz) cream

Half-fill a cocktail shaker with ice. Add the Galliano, crème de cacao and cream. Shake vigorously, then strain into a chilled cocktail glass.

It looks harmless enough, but this enticing creature comes with a nip in its tail.

stinger

ice cubes or crushed ice
45 ml (1½ oz) brandy
15 ml (½ oz) white crème de menthe
maraschino cherry

Place some ice cubes or crushed ice in a small highball glass. Add the brandy and crème de menthe and stir well. Garnish with a maraschino cherry.

stinger

A powerful home remedy for dirty rotten head colds. A cup before retiring and you won't feel a thing.

hot toddy

1 tablespoon soft brown sugar
4 slices of lemon
4 cinnamon sticks
12 whole cloves
125 ml (4 oz/1/2 cup) Scotch whisky

Put all the ingredients in a heatproof jug with 1 litre (35 oz/4 cups) boiling water. Stir, leave for a few minutes, then strain. Serve in heatproof glasses. Serves 4.

Ahoy there! Here's a rummy old trick to beat off the ills and chills of deepest, darkest winter.

buttered rum

1 tablespoon sugar
250 ml (9 oz/1 cup) rum
softened unsalted butter

Place the sugar, rum and 500 ml (17 oz/2 cups) boiling water in a heatproof jug. Stir to dissolve the sugar, then divide among four mugs. Stir 1–2 teaspoons of butter into each mug and enjoy hot. Serves 4.

virginal Sometimes it's perfectly acceptable to fake it — for instance when you have a headache from having had a little too much the evening before, or if you really must keep your wits about you. Sitting soft has never been such an appealing option with this memorable collection of marvellous mocktails. So there's really no reason why non-drinkers can't come to the party and have a smashing good time!

In these enlightened times we all know one must never drink and drive, so when a designated driver turns up on your doorstep with a gaggle of misfits intent on serious mischief, as a dutiful host it is incumbent on you to ensure our civic-minded friend isn't left entirely high and dry or at least empty handed! Of course, it isn't only drivers who need subtle diversions from inebriating pursuits. There are amongst our population certain abstemious types as well as those unruly, undisciplined souls who turn up at a party nursing rather dastardly hangovers and yet who can't quite manage to stay away! Thankfully, there are far more interesting creations than just boring soft drink to offer, or a tired old glass of tap water in which sits a sad squelch of lemon. Some of the spectacularly innocent mocktails gathered herein look just like the real thing, without the sting, so your non-drinking guests will arise with sparkling clear heads the next morning — unlike you, poor thing. Some you'll want to drink just for the sheer taste of it. What follows is a fine sprinkling of bubbly brews and luscious slushes and creamy delights you could enjoy any time of day. A great proportion of these mocktails are also astonishingly rejuvenating and bursting with nutrients — so don't be too surprised if you stumble upon a certain hangover remedy or two …

Cinderella scrubbed the floor and slept in the hearth but won a waistline to die for — oh, and a handsome prince.

cinderella

45 ml (1½ oz) orange juice
45 ml (1½ oz) pineapple juice
15 ml (½ oz) lemon juice
ice cubes

Pour the orange juice, pineapple juice and lemon juice into a cocktail shaker. Add a scoop of ice, shake vigorously, then strain into a chilled martini glass.

Bring a dimple to the cheeks of whoever's steering the good ship lollipop home tonight.

shirley temple

ice cubes
good dash of grenadine
ginger ale or lemonade
30 ml (1 oz) cream
maraschino cherries

Place some ice in a tall glass, add the grenadine and top with ginger ale or lemonade. Float the cream on top over the back of a teaspoon. Garnish with maraschino cherries and serve with a straw and a swizzle stick.

cinderella

Give tired tastebuds the razzle dazzle treatment.

sweet tang

150 g (5¹/2 oz/1 cup) fresh strawberries or raspberries
125 ml (4 oz/¹/2 cup) cranberry juice

Place the berries and cranberry juice in a blender and blend until smooth.
Pour into a medium glass.

BARTENDER'S TIP If fresh berries aren't in season, use frozen instead.

A citrus sling with a ring of sweetness.

lemonade

egg white
caster (superfine) sugar
juice of 1 lemon
juice of 1 lime
soda water
sugar syrup

Dip the rim of two medium glasses in a saucer of egg white, then a saucer of sugar, shaking off any excess. Chill the glasses. Mix the lemon juice and lime juice together in a jug. Pour into the sugar-frosted glasses, then top up with soda water. Stir in sugar syrup to taste.

lemonade

A beautiful drink that does wonders for the complexion.

blushing peach

125 ml (4 oz/¹/₂ cup) peach juice
125 ml (4 oz/¹/₂ cup) almond milk
good dash of Angostura bitters
ice cubes
drizzle of grenadine

Combine the peach juice, almond milk and bitters in a cocktail shaker with five large cubes of ice. Shake well, then strain into a medium glass. Drizzle with a little grenadine and use the tip of a knife to gently swirl the grenadine into a pretty pattern.

So simple, so yummy, who needs dessert?

egg nog

1 egg
1/2 teaspoon pure vanilla extract
2 teaspoons caster (superfine) sugar
125 ml (4 oz/1/2 cup) cream
125 ml (4 oz/1/2 cup) milk
large pinch freshly grated nutmeg, plus extra for sprinkling
3 large ice cubes

Crack the egg into a heavy-duty blender and add the vanilla, sugar, cream, milk, nutmeg and ice cubes. Blend until smooth and frothy. Pour into a medium glass and sprinkle with a little extra grated nutmeg.

blushing peach

An entertaining, all-American classic.

mickey mouse

ice cubes
cola
1 scoop vanilla ice cream
whipped cream
3 maraschino cherries

Place some ice in a tall glass. Add enough cola to two-thirds fill the glass, then float a scoop of ice cream on top, then some whipped cream. Garnish with maraschino cherries.

A bittersweet reminder of all those happy days.

cherry cola

ice cubes
125 ml (4 oz/1/2 cup) vanilla-flavoured cola
125 ml (4 oz/1/2 cup) sour cherry juice
maraschino cherry, with stem

Place some ice cubes in a tall glass. Combine the cola and cherry juice and
pour into the glass. Garnish with a maraschino cherry.

alphabetical index

207

Published in 2010 by Murdoch Books Pty Limited

Murdoch Books Australia
Pier 8/9, 23 Hickson Road
Millers Point NSW 2000
Phone: +61 (0)2 8220 2000
Fax: +61 (0)2 8220 2558
www.murdochbooks.com.au

Murdoch Books UK Limited
Erico House, 6th Floor
93–99 Upper Richmond Road
Putney, London SW15 2TG
Phone: +44 (0)20 8785 5995
Fax: +44 (0)20 8785 5985
www.murdochbooks.co.uk

Chief Executive: Juliet Rogers

Publisher: Lynn Lewis
Senior Designer: Heather Menzies
Design Layout: Handpress Graphics
Editorial Coordinator: Liz Malcolm
Production: Joan Beal

National Library of Australia Cataloguing-in-Publication Data
Title: Cocktails. ISBN: 978-1-74196-947-4 (pbk.)
Series: New chubbie. Notes: Includes index. Subjects: Cocktails. Dewey Number: 641.874

Printed by 1010 Printing International.
PRINTED IN CHINA

IMPORTANT: Those who might be at risk from the effects of salmonella poisoning (the elderly, pregnant women, young children and those suffering from immune deficiency diseases) should consult their doctor with any concerns about eating raw eggs.

OVEN GUIDE: You may find cooking times vary depending on the oven you are using. For fan-forced ovens, as a general rule, set the oven temperature to 20°C (35°F) lower than indicated in the recipe.